THE AFTER-TRAUMA NOTEBOOK
Written Exposure Therapy to Process, Release, and Heal

A five-week guided program designed by therapists to lead you through Written Exposure Therapy, a first-line treatment for reprocessing trauma.

. . . .

(THIS BOOK BELONGS TO)

. . . .

(IF FOUND, PLEASE RETURN TO)

LEARN MORE
www.therapynotebooks.com

THERAPY NOTEBOOKS
Published by Subject Matters

ISBN: 9781958963999
Printed in the USA

LEAD THERAPISTS
Jessica Yu, PhD
Diana Hu, PsyD

EDITED BY
Hod Tamir, PhD

DESIGNED BY
Monumento.Co

BRANDING BY
High Tide

IF YOU ARE IN URGENT
NEED OF ASSISTANCE:
Dial 9-1-1

FOR MENTAL HEALTH
CRISIS SUPPORT:
Dial 9-8-8

SAMHSA National Helpline
1-800-622-HELP (4357)

Crisis Text Line
Text HOME to 741741

Welcome and a Note on Being Careful

A significant part of working through difficult or traumatic memories is purposefully, and carefully, moving through triggering memories. This notebook is inspired by Written Exposure Therapy, which is safe and well-researched, but the original treatment protocol requires the work to be done in-person with a clinician. In this book, you may be working on your own. Though we have done our best to adapt the research to this format, it's important to know that this process may still become difficult, and it may be beneficial to remain attentive toward how you're feeling.

Here are resources that may help:

- *To find grounding and calm after or between sessions:*
  Appendix A: Distress Tolerance Techniques

- *For answers to common questions:*
  Appendix B: Frequently Asked Questions

- *For immediate assistance from a trained professional:*
  SAMHSA National Helpline
  1-800-622-HELP (4357)

  National Suicide Prevention Lifeline
  Dial 9-8-8

  Crisis Text Line
  Text HOME to 741741

This book is not a replacement for therapy or direct work with a professional. We do our best to provide access to some of the most effective and evidence-based tools that clinicians trust. If you're interested in and have access to therapy, we encourage you to contact a professional.

Note on Written Exposure Therapy

Written Exposure Therapy has been shown to be effective when practiced with a clinician; however, it has yet to be thoroughly tested in a book or self-help format. Therefore, this is not a replacement for conducting Written Exposure Therapy or other therapy with a professional.

The main writing prompts in this book come directly from the official treatment manual for Written Exposure Therapy. We received copyright permissions and licensing from the American Psychological Association, but the APA or the researchers in no way endorse this book.

The clinicians who helped write and edit this book have done their best to present the Written Exposure Therapy prompts and procedure as tested in research while adapting it to fit the format of this book. They did so based on their training and what they believed would be helpful, safe, and effective.

Even though this specific book has not been endorsed by the protocol authors or tested on its own, we believe it could still help people in need. We know not everyone has the time, money, or energy to find professional assistance. Through our notebooks, we hope to make well-researched, effective treatments accessible to more people.

Letter From a Therapist

As a clinician, I'm often told about the worst days of a person's life. One of the first patients I ever worked with was a woman who lost her young son in a house fire. For years after, she remained in the same community, in the same job, walking the same roads. What she really wanted—and needed—was change. She wanted to move to a state where she had more family. She wanted to find a job that would give her a sense of meaning. She wanted the prospect of a new romantic relationship. But, defined as she was by the deeply tragic trauma she'd suffered, she couldn't fathom making these things happen.

When we talk about trauma, we often focus on the physical and psychological symptoms—agitation, flashbacks, interrupted sleep—but what I've found to be the most potent and wrenching impact of trauma is how it can paralyze those who experience it. Trauma keeps us locked in a constant state of vigilance, with little space left for the creativity, joy, and motivation required to build a meaningful future.

Clinically, trauma means something specific: the Diagnostic and Statistical Manual of Mental Disorders, Fifth Edition (DSM-5), defines it as experiencing or witnessing "actual or threatened death, serious injury, or sexual violence."[1] But trauma can be any extraordinarily distressing event that shatters a person's sense of security and safety. In fact, 70 percent of adults in the U.S. will experience some kind of traumatic event in their lifetime.[2] While the clinical definition is important, any trauma we experience deserves to be treated as worthy of attention and care.

Thankfully, researchers and clinicians have made great strides in understanding the biology of trauma and developing treatments. One of the most effective treatments is exposure therapy, which asks you to vividly recall the traumatic event and exposes you to trauma triggers in a therapeutic environment in order to reprocess them. In doing so, you give your brain the opportunity to feel safe, and to incorporate new ways of understanding your experience.

As a clinician, I've seen firsthand the transformative effects of confronting your trauma. Through exposure protocols—like the one included in this notebook—my patient whose life had been so catastrophically altered in the house fire was able to move to a new city to be closer to her family, and when we last spoke, she was taking concrete steps to build a life less defined by her trauma. She sounded so much lighter and happier.

Seeking help for trauma, regardless of how long ago the experience occurred, shows courage, resilience, and strength. In opening this notebook, you are imagining a better future. Trusting in the process—and in yourself—is the first step in regaining power over your trauma. I am honored to be part of that journey.

Sincerely,

Dr. Jessica Yu, with assistance from Dr. Diana Hu
Lead Clinicians

Scan the QR code to
meet our clinicians

How This Book Helps You

1   Structured journaling to help you process and release a
     traumatic memory.

     Confronting trauma is one of the most difficult things we can
     do, and it is almost impossible without support. We provide the
     structure to help you gently confront your traumatic memory so
     you can move forward without fear.

2   Experience a first-line, evidence-based treatment in a self-guided
     format.

     We've translated Written Exposure Therapy, a treatment used
     extensively by the United States Department of Veteran Affairs
     for trauma and PTSD, into notebook form to make it accessible
     to you.

3   Find the language for your trauma.

     Trauma is often made up of little more than frightening
     fragments and unhelpful associations. We help you rewrite your
     trauma narrative to give new meaning to your experience.

4   Clear guidance every step of the way.

     Trauma can make you feel alone in your experience, but our
     expert therapists hold your hand throughout the process with
     notes, tips, and step-by-step instructions so you'll always have
     someone to lean on.

5   Made by therapists committed to making evidence-based tools
     more accessible.

     We know that seeking professional support isn't always possible.
     The therapists behind this notebook are passionate about
     making healing available to all, so you can do this work on your
     own schedule, when it makes sense for you.

Contents

INTRODUCTION:
On Trauma and Written Exposure Therapy

WHAT IS TRAUMA?

Our minds are a vast, labyrinthian collection of memories and experiences: when I sit on a bike, I remember to balance; when I see a certain face, I say 'Alice'; when I smell pizza, I salivate. We see, we smell, we feel, we hear, and we associate: we link two things together, sometimes consciously, sometimes automatically.

When the brain and body sense danger, for example, our heart rate increases. Blood rushes to the brain, our senses sharpen, and our muscles prime for fight or flight. These stress responses are unconscious, immediate, and necessary: if a threat is present, we need to be equipped to handle it.

But what happens when there is no threat? A song that was playing on the radio when you crashed your car; the smell of the meal you were cooking when you received devastating news. These cues, harmless in any other context, are red warning lights to your nervous system, which is designed to protect you—even when it doesn't need to.

Our brains learn through association, automatically linking together stimuli with memories. The tang of mint leaves makes us think of our grandmother, even when she's hundreds of miles away. When associative memories are formed in response to stressors, this is known as threat conditioning (previously called "fear conditioning").[3] Threat conditioning is an evolutionary advantage—burn your hand on the stove, and you'll know to avoid it in the future. In the case of associated memories formed with trauma, however, our brains may associate otherwise neutral stimuli with danger. If our trauma involves an ambulance, any siren may be read as a threat and trigger our stress response, even when we are entirely safe.

People who experience trauma symptoms often feel frustrated or ashamed that they can't reason their way out of it ("I know that siren isn't coming for me, so why am I panicking?"). But it's the natural connectivity of our brain that makes it so difficult.

The deeper, primal parts of the brain—the thalamus, amygdala, and hippocampus—are in constant communication, processing sensory information, assessing threats, managing fear, and shaping our deepest, most potent memories. Information travels quickly here. When you hear a sound, the auditory signal takes two paths: one is a shortcut straight from the thalamus to your threat-sensing amygdala; the other is a slower but more precise route through your higher-level cortex. Studies show it takes nearly twice as long for the information to be processed by brain regions responsible for conscious reasoning and language than for the information to shortcut from the thalamus to the amygdala.[4] This particular organization of the brain is vital when survival depends on split-second reactions, but it is also why traumatic memories can be so difficult to work through. Even when we consciously know we're not in danger, it's difficult to stop our body from reacting as if we are.

Sometimes, even attempting to talk about or process trauma can feel impossible. Trauma sufferers describe being unable to recall key details of the experience, or being overwhelmed by waves of seemingly disconnected memories and emotions. In his research, pioneering trauma scholar Dr. Bessel van der Kolk found that when monitoring brain scans of patients with PTSD, activity in the part of the brain normally associated with language dramatically decreased.[5][6] People were feeling, but not processing, the experience of intense associative memories that had cemented beyond their conscious reach.

Unfortunately, too, trauma responses become biologically and psychologically more intense over time. The shock and cortisol that course through the body when confronted with triggers lead us to avoid the triggers entirely. But avoidance perpetuates our inability to process, and worsens the shame and guilt around the original experience. The shame and guilt then increase our avoidance, and the cycle goes frustratingly on. And yet our brains, for all their tricky misfiring, are also incredibly resilient and dynamic. We now know the brain is constantly changing, even throughout adulthood; different types of treatment and psychotherapy actually affect its structure and function. Not only that, you are capable of learning new thought patterns and coping skills to replace the ones you were taught by trauma.

WRITTEN EXPOSURE THERAPY

Neuroscientists, psychiatrists, and clinicians have all reached a similar consensus over the last few decades of research: avoidance makes trauma worse, and while confronting those memories can be difficult, it is required for change. This knowledge underlies one of the latest evidence-based treatments for trauma, Written Exposure Therapy (WET).[7] Written Exposure Therapy uses five sessions of journaling to address the trauma response in two key ways: first, by asking patients to explore the traumatic event in a safe, therapeutic environment, it "rewires" the neural pathways and creates new, less triggering associative memories; and second, by allowing patients to reprocess the event and see their trauma in a more meaningful and more holistic light.[8]

The process of re-exploring trauma memories and triggers in order to override the fear or threat response is called threat extinction, and it teaches the amygdala that the trigger is no longer cause for alarm. This enables us to feel more secure in the world and less anxious about confronting sense memories—and that biological security allows us to move toward the conscious processing of the traumatic event. In WET, this is done through expressive writing.

If expressive writing—journaling, essentially—hasn't been part of your practice of self-care, it might feel strange, even silly, to start. Yet study after study shows that exploring your deepest and most powerful thoughts and feelings through writing contributes to everything from improved memory to a stronger immune system.[9][10] Writing about trauma, in particular, has been shown to actually alleviate trauma symptoms.[11] Getting your thoughts and fears out of your head and onto the page gives your brain a "break" from continually processing and ruminating on the trauma, which in turn enables better sleep and improved mood. Recent trials have shown Written Exposure Therapy to be as or more effective than one of the most commonly prescribed trauma therapies, Cognitive Processing Therapy.[12] It has even been adopted as a "first-line" treatment for PTSD by the U.S. Department of Veterans Affairs due to its efficacy, low dropout rates, and ease of implementation.

Written Exposure Therapy asks you to do something immensely difficult: to vividly recall your traumatic experience, to relive the pain, and to revisit emotions and memories you've learned to avoid. Yet it is in facing those difficulties that you find your power. You learn you can confront your trauma without being defined by it; that your trauma, as painful as it was, also led you to this place of profound strength, knowledge, and tenderness.

Note From
a Therapist

Confronting traumatic experiences takes courage and we applaud you for your willingness to do so. Before beginning your writing sessions, we'd like to offer some words of encouragement and wisdom.

CONFRONTING RATHER THAN AVOIDING

It won't be easy, but in order to get the most out of this book, be prepared to fully confront the difficult memories, thoughts, and feelings around your traumatic experience. Avoidance is a very natural and often helpful coping mechanism. It can feel good in the short term, but reinforces our beliefs that certain associations continue to be dangerous. When we avoid, we don't get to learn that we are safe now, and it is okay now.

If you feel yourself straying from your memory as you write, pull yourself back in. And remember: though you may be reliving the memory, you are no longer there, and you are safe now.

PREPARING FOR SOME DISCOMFORT

The writing sessions ahead will be difficult, and the first few sessions especially so, because you may be used to avoiding your trauma. You may even experience a temporary increase in anxiety, agitation, and flashbacks. This is normal. Over time, through continued writing, you will gain a sense of control over your trauma, learn to make meaning from it, and experience a decrease in symptoms. Stick with it while you can, but be attentive to your limits: physical illness, overwhelming life demands, and other major stressors can impact the energy you have to write. Do what you need to make this work for you.

Preparation

SELECT A SINGLE MEMORY
TO WRITE ABOUT

Focusing on a single highly distressing memory throughout the five writing sessions is one of the most important components of the work.

•   Choose the Most Vivid, Stressful, Specific Moment

The more significant and vivid the memory, the greater the healing impact of your writing. If you have experienced more than one traumatic event, choose the one that causes you the most distress (it's likely the one that you've most tried to avoid). If you experienced something that occurred over an extended period of time, start with a single episode or memory within that period that causes you the greatest distress. If many memories feel equally distressing to you, choose one of which you have the most vivid and clear memory, where you can most clearly identify what happened, where, when, and who was involved. If you can only remember certain parts of an event, that's okay. Focus on the parts you remember.

•   Recount from Beginning (When You Sensed Fear) to End

Choosing an appropriate moment in time within your memory will also improve the impact of your writing. By "appropriate moment," we mean the part of your traumatic experience that was most activating or distressing. This helps ensure you are not inadvertently avoiding your trauma by writing about parts that are not as activating or distressing.

    That being said, we do not want you to overthink where to begin and where to end your memory. Consider the following guidance if you need help defining that appropriate moment. However, keep in mind that your traumatic memory is your traumatic memory. What you consider the most activating and distressing part can only be determined by you, not arbitrary rules.

Start at the moment you sensed fear, distress, or danger. End at the moment you sensed greater safety or felt the adrenaline rush start to subside. This is often when the physical threat of danger ends (like when you walk away from a dangerous situation, when a traumatic conversation finishes, or when a threatening person has finally left). If the trauma you experienced was not a physical threat, it may be when you subjectively felt much safer.

For example, if you choose to write about a car accident, you may begin with when you first sensed danger as the other car got too close. And you may end with when you felt you were no longer in acute physical danger, which may be when you exited the car or when you first made contact with paramedics. An extremely intense confrontation may also be considered a traumatic experience. If you sensed danger or fear the moment a person walked in the room, this is where you would begin. However, if you only sensed danger or fear after noticing certain verbal or physical cues, then begin there. And again, end with when you felt the danger was no longer present, you began to feel safe, and your adrenaline subsided. This may be as soon as they left the room, or only after you felt certain they had left the building. The sense of acute danger and safety can be subjective, but those can serve as your beginning and end.

If you choose to write about a trauma that you witnessed as a first responder, observer, or acquaintance, you may begin with when you first arrived on the scene and observed danger. End with when you were done tending to the victim or no longer sensed the danger right in front of you.

- You May Choose Another Memory After the First Five Weeks

If there are multiple memories you'd like to work through, that is okay. After focusing on a single memory during your first five weeks, feel free to use the same questions for another five weeks of writing, focused on a different memory and moment in time.

It may be challenging to select only one memory. You can use the next
three pages to jot down memories that you may want to write about,
and note what comes up for you. From there, narrow in on which
memory elicits the most distress and is vivid enough for you to explore
in detail for the next five weeks.

SCHEDULE 45 MINUTES PER WEEK

Each week, schedule 45 minutes to devote to your writing session. You'll spend the first 5 minutes getting settled, the next 30 minutes writing about your traumatic experience, and the final 5–10 minutes checking in and getting grounded.

We recommend scheduling your writing session as you would any other appointment. Having a consistent and dedicated time to write helps you follow through with the protocol and maintain progress over time. Mark a time on your calendar every week for the next five weeks. Weekly consistency is an important part of WET working well, so please do this before continuing.

SET UP A COMFORTABLE SPACE

Find a comfortable, private, and safe space for yourself that will be available to you during these sessions. Make sure your space will be free of distractions: no TV, cell phones, laptops, or any noises, people, or objects that may draw your attention away from your writing.

You will also need a timer or alarm clock. It's best if you have a separate timer; if you plan to rely on your phone or another smart device as a timer, make sure it is on airplane mode or set for complete silence.

WHAT TO EXPECT: CHECK-INS AND WRITING PROMPTS

• Check in at the Beginning and End of Writing

Immediately before and after writing, you will check in on how you're feeling through what clinicians call the Subjective Units of Distress, or SUDs, scale. This rating serves as a quick way to measure change over the five weeks and possibly adjust your writing approach as needed. On a scale of 1–10, you'll log how distressed you're feeling: 0 is so relaxed you could fall asleep and 10 is the most stressed you've ever felt in your life.

• Write with the Exact Research Prompts

We'll be presenting certain instructions and prompts directly from the research to help ensure the highest treatment efficacy. We received copyright permission from the American Psychological Association to provide this for you. We're very excited you will have direct access to this research. At times you may notice a slightly different format and tone.

The next and final portion of the preparation section is an introduction to Written Exposure Therapy, directly from the researchers.

Introduction to Written Exposure Therapy

From Written Exposure Therapy for PTSD: A Brief Treatment Approach for Mental Health Professionals (p. 94), by D. M. Sloan and B. P. Marx, 2019, Washington, DC: American Psychological Association. Copyright 2019 by the American Psychological Association.

Survivors of traumatic experiences often go through changes in their physical reactions, emotions, thoughts, and behaviors in the wake of such experiences.

Examples of changes in physical reactions may include increased fatigue, nausea (feeling sick to your stomach), sweating or chills, shock, dizziness, chest pains, trouble breathing, and numbness.

Examples of emotional changes may include increased nervousness, fear, grief, depression, hopelessness, helplessness, anger, irritability, feeling overwhelmed, guilt, and vulnerability.

Examples of changes in thinking may include increased thinking that your future will be cut short, difficulty in remembering things, trouble making decisions, confusion, difficulty concentrating, "flashbacks" or reliving experiences, nightmares, intrusive or unwelcome thoughts, too many thoughts at once, thinking about suicide, and memory gaps.

Examples of changes in behavior may include increased startle, hypervigilance, being withdrawn from others, being overly dependent upon others, changes in appetite, changes in sleep, increased substance abuse (alcohol, drugs, medication), problems with emotional or physical intimacy, inability to trust or have loving feelings, apathy, loss of spirituality, risk taking, and suicidal impulses and behaviors.

Each person may differ in the ways in which these reactions are experienced. Some may be very familiar but others may not. Many of these reactions become part of the trauma survivor's everyday life and do not seem unusual to him or her. Take a moment to think about how many of the above symptoms you experienced since the traumatic event.

The manner in which a survivor attempts to cope with his or her trauma symptoms also has an impact on everyday activities. If a trauma survivor has recurring thoughts and memories of a trauma, they may attempt to avoid them by using substances (alcohol and/or drugs), becoming a workaholic, staying away from other people, or using anger and aggressive behavior to either distract oneself or remove any reminders of the trauma from the current circumstances. These strategies may give the trauma survivor short-term relief but over the long-term can be problematic for a variety of reasons. In other words, sometimes a survivor's attempt to cure or to cope with reactions to a traumatic event can become a problem in and of itself.

Importantly, approaches that one might use to deal with nontraumatic events do not work very well in dealing with trauma. People will sometimes tell trauma survivors to "forget about it" and to get on with their lives. This approach may work well in many different situations, but one does not just forget about traumatic events.

One of the reasons that this advice does not work is that events that are experienced as traumatic are remembered differently from nontraumatic events. The memory of a trauma may be stored in a splintered fashion as a protection from reexperiencing the full impact of the trauma. Consequently, survivors may have amnesia for large segments of time surrounding the trauma. Or they may remember some details of past traumas but may not have any feelings attached to these memories. They may experience overwhelming anxiety or fearfulness without understanding the cause. Certain situations may trigger "flashbacks" to earlier traumas, and they might feel that they are actually reliving the past.

To successfully recover from the traumatic event, it is important that you confront that experience by recounting it, repeatedly, in as much detail and with as much emotion as possible. By repeatedly recounting the event, you will be able to correct for the splintered fashion in which the memory may have been stored. You will also find that recounting the experience will result in you feeling like you have more control over the memory rather than feeling as if the memory controls you. Over the next several sessions, I will be asking you to repeatedly recount the trauma experience by writing about the experience.

WEEK I

Note From
a Therapist

As you begin your first writing session, remember to get settled in a comfortable, private, and distraction-free space, and to set a timer for 30 minutes. Commit to writing about your traumatic experience. Be sure to write in the past tense. Research currently shows people are better able to accurately recount and work through distressing memories when using the past tense.[13][14]

As you'll read in the first writing prompt, you'll be asked to start from the moment you realized something awful was about to happen and to engage your five senses in order to recall the memory more vividly. All of this will enable you to activate your memory and access events, thoughts, and feelings that you may have been avoiding for some time.

You may not finish writing about the entire trauma in this session. That is okay. Focus on remembering and writing in as much detail as possible, rather than trying to finish recalling the entire memory in one sitting. If you finish before the 30 minutes are up, start again from the beginning until your timer goes off, trying to remember any details or feelings you may have missed.

If you feel yourself becoming very distressed during writing, know that there will be time at the end of your 30 minutes to recalibrate and ground yourself. Keep writing. It is undoubtedly difficult—and meaningful—work.

REMINDERS

- Choose a single, specific memory. The more distressing and vivid, the greater impact your writing will have.

- Write in the past tense, engage all five senses, and recall all the thoughts and feelings you had at the time of your traumatic experience.

- Keep writing for the full 30 minutes. It may feel very difficult, but you'll have an opportunity to ground yourself at the end.

Writing Session 1 Prompt

From Written Exposure Therapy, by Sloan and Marx, 2019,
Washington, DC: APA. Copyright 2019 by the APA.

Over the next five sessions I would like you to write about your trauma. Don't worry about your spelling or grammar. I would like you to write about the details of the trauma as you remember it now—for example, how the trauma event happened and whether other people were involved. In writing about the details of the trauma, it is important to write about specifics of what happened and what you were feeling and thinking as the trauma was happening. Try to be as specific in recounting the details as possible. It is also important that you really let go and explore your very deepest emotions and thoughts about the trauma. You should also keep in mind that you have five sessions to write about this experience, so you don't need to be concerned with completing your account of the trauma within today's session. Just be sure to be as detailed about the trauma as possible and also to write about your thoughts and feelings as you remember them during (and immediately after) the trauma.

For your first writing session, I'd like you to write about the trauma starting at the beginning. For instance, you could begin with the moment you realized the trauma was about to happen. As you describe the trauma, it is important that you provide as many specific details as you can remember. For example, you might write about what you saw (e.g., headlights of the car approaching you, person approaching you), what you heard (e.g., car horn, screeching tires, person threatening you, explosion), or what you smelled (e.g., blood, burning rubber). In addition to writing about the details of the trauma, you should also be writing about your thoughts and feelings during the trauma as you remember it now.

For example, you might have had the thought, "I'm going to die," "This can't be happening," or "I'm going to be raped." And you might have felt terrified, frozen with fear, or angry at another person involved.

Remember, you don't need to finish writing about the entire trauma in this session. Just focus on writing about the trauma with as much detail as possible and include the thoughts and feelings you experienced during and immediately after the trauma. Remember, the trauma is not actually happening again, you are simply recounting it as you look back upon it now.

Before you begin writing:

1. Check-In: How distressed are you feeling in this moment before writing? (0 = not at all, 10 = the most I ever felt)

2. Set your 30-minute timer, and when you're ready, begin your timer and begin writing.

If you need more space to write there are a few extra pages at the end. Once time is up, please remember to measure how you feel below.

Post-Writing Check-In: How distressed are you feeling in this moment?
(0 = not at all, 10 = the most I ever felt)

Take a moment to transition your mind from the memory to reflecting on your writing experience. Ten minutes is about the right
amount of time for the next section. If you need to, ground yourself
in the present moment by using each of your five senses to notice
something about the room you are in, or refer to Appendix A for
more techniques.

Wrap-Up and Transition

Writing reflection: How did the writing feel? What was difficult or
challenging about it? Did you remember more than you expected?
Remember: do not continue writing about the memory; reflect only
on the writing process itself.

CONCLUDING NOTE

*From Written Exposure Therapy, by Sloan and Marx, 2019, Washington, DC: APA.
Copyright 2019 by the APA.*

You will likely have thoughts, images, and feelings concerning the
trauma you just wrote about during the course of the upcoming
week. It is important that you allow yourself to have these
thoughts, images, and feelings, whatever they might be, rather
than trying to push them away. Please try to allow yourself to have
whatever thoughts, images, and feelings that may come up.

WEEK II

Note From
a Therapist

Since your last writing session you may be feeling more distressed or having more flashbacks than usual. This is normal. You've been pulling up all the memories, thoughts, and feelings that you've been burying for weeks, months, or years. Be proud of yourself for allowing these experiences to come up and working through them. These difficult sensations are an indication that you are fully engaged in your writing and allowing a new integration of your trauma experience.

As you prepare for your second writing session, it may be helpful to remind yourself of how to focus your writing. Look back at last week's writing and check:

- Did you write about the specific traumatic memory that is most distressing or most clear?

- Did you focus on a single moment in time, starting from the moment you sensed danger to the moment the acute danger passed?

- Did you write about the specific details of the distressing event itself, including your deepest thoughts and feelings as the event occurred?

This week, you'll focus on diving deeper into what happened by digging into your deepest feelings and thoughts as the event transpired.

REMINDERS

- Make sure you're focusing on a single, specific, highly distressing event. It may be helpful to look back at last week's writing and check.

- These first few writing sessions may feel particularly distressing—it's okay to be checking in at 8, 9, or 10. Do your best to stick with it.

Writing Session 2 Prompt

From Written Exposure Therapy, by Sloan and Marx, 2019, Washington, DC: APA. Copyright 2019 by the APA.

Today, I want you to continue to write about the trauma as you look back upon it now. If you feel that you didn't get the chance to completely describe the trauma in the last writing session, then you can pick up where you left off. If you completed writing about the trauma event in the last session, please write about the entire trauma again. While you are describing the trauma, I really want you to delve into your very deepest feelings (e.g., fear, shock, sadness, anger) and thoughts (e.g., "Is this really happening?" "I'm going to die"). Also, remember to write about the details of the trauma. That is, describe the setting; the people involved; and what you saw, heard, and felt. Remember that you are writing about the trauma as you look back upon it now.

Before you begin writing:

1. Check-In: How distressed are you feeling in this moment before writing?
(0 = not at all, 10 = the most I ever felt)

2. Set your 30-minute timer, and when you're ready, begin your timer and begin writing.

If you need more space to write there are a few extra pages at the end. Once time is up, please remember to measure how you feel below.

Post-Writing Check-In: How distressed are you feeling in this moment?
(0 = not at all, 10 = the most I ever felt)

Take a moment to transition your mind from the memory to reflecting on your writing experience. Ten minutes is about the right
amount of time for the next section. If you need to, ground yourself
in the present moment by using each of your five senses to notice
something about the room you are in, or refer to Appendix A for
more techniques.

Wrap-Up and Transition

Writing reflection: How did the writing feel? What was difficult or
challenging about it? Did you remember more than you expected?
Remember: do not continue writing about the memory; reflect only
on the writing process itself.

CONCLUDING NOTE

*From Written Exposure Therapy, by Sloan and Marx, 2019, Washington, DC: APA.
Copyright 2019 by the APA.*

As I've stated previously, you will likely have thoughts, feelings,
and visual images concerning the trauma during the course of the
upcoming week. It is important that you allow yourself to have
these thoughts, images, and feelings, whatever they might be,
rather than trying to push them away. Please try to allow yourself
to have whatever thoughts, images, and feelings that come up.

WEEK III

Note From
a Therapist

The most difficult part of working through traumatic experiences is having to confront and feel the deeply painful feelings you'd rather leave in the past. We want to reiterate that this is a necessary part of the process and encourage you to continue this difficult work.

If you notice your feelings about the event are beginning to seem less intense, that's wonderful; it indicates your brain is starting to learn that this memory is not something that has to be feared. Continue to work through the most distressing parts of the memory and keep the progress going.

If your stress levels are about the same, that's okay, too. As you write this week, try to focus on the little details of what you were thinking and feeling during the event; describe your experience as clearly as possible. If you begin sensing mental resistance, you're in the right place: pause and notice the resistance, take a breath, and keep writing.

This week you'll also start what clinicians call the "processing" component of the work. By writing about the details of the event, your brain likely has already begun associating safer feelings with the memory. By processing the impact of this event on your life, you'll start to integrate it into how you understand yourself. You'll reflect on how your experience may have changed your life and any meaning you may have already made from it. This is a critical step in nearly all forms of trauma treatment and a significant part of your writing.

REMINDERS

- Make sure to stay focused on the same single memory as the last two weeks (you'll have a chance at the end to explore more memories).

- Nudge yourself to explore the parts of the memory that you might resist remembering. Write for the full 30 minutes.

- Prepare to begin deeper processing: how has the experience impacted your life?

Writing Session 3 Prompt

From Written Exposure Therapy, by Sloan and Marx, 2019, Washington, DC: APA. Copyright 2019 by the APA.

In your writing today, I again want you to continue writing about the trauma event as you think about it today. If you have completed writing about the entire trauma you experienced, you can either write about the trauma again from the beginning or you can select a part of the trauma that is most upsetting to you and focus your writing on that specific part of the experience. In addition, I would also like you to begin to write about how the traumatic experience has changed your life. For instance, you might write about whether or not the trauma has changed the way you view your life, the meaning of life, and how you relate to other people. Throughout your writing, I want you to really let go and write about your deepest thoughts and feelings.

Before you begin writing:

1. Check-In: How distressed are you feeling in this moment before writing? (0 = not at all, 10 = the most I ever felt)

2. Set your 30-minute timer, and when you're ready, begin your timer and begin writing.

If you need more space to write there are a few extra pages at the end. Once time is up, please remember to measure how you feel below.

Post-Writing Check-In: How distressed are you feeling in this moment?
(0 = not at all, 10 = the most I ever felt)

Take a moment to transition your mind from the memory to reflecting on your writing experience. Ten minutes is about the right
amount of time for the next section. If you need to, ground yourself
in the present moment by using each of your five senses to notice
something about the room you are in, or refer to Appendix A for
more techniques.

Wrap-Up and Transition

Writing reflection: How did the writing feel? What was difficult or
challenging about it? Did you remember more than you expected?
Remember: do not continue writing about the memory; reflect only
on the writing process itself.

CONCLUDING NOTE

*From Written Exposure Therapy, by Sloan and Marx, 2019, Washington, DC: APA.
Copyright 2019 by the APA.*

As I've stated previously, you will likely have thoughts, feelings,
and visual images concerning the trauma during the course of the
upcoming week. It is important that you allow yourself to have
these thoughts, images, and feelings, whatever they might be,
rather than trying to push them away. Please try to allow yourself
to have whatever thoughts, images, and feelings that come up.

WEEK IV

Note From a Therapist

This will be your second-to-last writing session. You'll be asked to process and reflect even more deeply. Be prepared to consider all the ways your selected memory has impacted your life: think about what new beliefs you have now about how you should behave or how much you can depend on others. Think about how it's impacted your decisions, the values you've upheld, and the people you've surrounded yourself with. Finally, consider how it has affected how you view yourself.

If you have any trouble articulating or reflecting on the impact of your selected traumatic event, think about what "rules" you have set for yourself that may stem from the event: for instance,"I always have to be prepared and rely primarily on myself," "I can't share too much with others because it could be used against me," "I can't wear certain things because it'll make me a target," or "I can't get too close or attached to people, because they might be taken from me."

In identifying what these impacts, thoughts, or rules are, you have the opportunity to choose whether these are helpful and effective to maintain, or whether you want to challenge or refute them.

REMINDERS

- Make sure to continue with the same single memory as the last few weeks, recalling in the past tense.

- Prepare to reflect deeply on how the experience has shaped your sense of self, others, and the world.

- Write for the full 30 minutes, even if you have to start from the beginning.

Writing Session 4 Prompt

From Written Exposure Therapy, by Sloan and Marx, 2019, Washington, DC: APA. Copyright 2019 by the APA.

I want you to continue to write about the trauma today. As with your writing in the last session, you can select a specific part of the trauma to write about; that is, the part of the trauma that was most upsetting to you. Today, I would also like you to write about how the trauma event has changed your life. You might write about if the trauma has changed the way you view your life, the meaning of life, and how you relate to other people. Throughout the session I want you to really let go and write about your deepest thoughts and feelings.

Before you begin writing:

1. Check-In: How distressed are you feeling in this moment before writing?
(0 = not at all, 10 = the most I ever felt)

2. Set your 30-minute timer, and when you're ready, begin your timer and begin writing.

If you need more space to write there are a few extra pages at the end. Once time is up, please remember to measure how you feel below.

Post-Writing Check-In: How distressed are you feeling in this moment?
(0 = not at all, 10 = the most I ever felt)

Take a moment to transition your mind from the memory to reflecting on your writing experience. Ten minutes is about the right
amount of time for the next section. If you need to, ground yourself
in the present moment by using each of your five senses to notice
something about the room you are in, or refer to Appendix A for
more techniques.

Wrap-Up and Transition

Writing reflection: How did the writing feel? What was difficult or challenging about it? Did you remember more than you expected? Remember: do not continue writing about the memory; reflect only on the writing process itself.

CONCLUDING NOTE

From Written Exposure Therapy, by Sloan and Marx, 2019, Washington, DC: APA. Copyright 2019 by the APA.

As I've stated previously, you will likely have thoughts, feelings, and visual images concerning the trauma during the course of the upcoming week. It is important that you allow yourself to have these thoughts, images, and feelings, whatever they might be, rather than trying to push them away. Please try to allow yourself to have whatever thoughts, images, and feelings that come up.

WEEK V

Note From
a Therapist

You have made it to your final writing session. This is no small feat. It required insight to understand the impact trauma was having on your life, willingness to open this journal, and courage and commitment to write about your experience week after week.

As you'll see in this week's prompt, you will focus on "wrapping up" your writing. Write about how it has affected your life, how it is connected to the person you are today, and how it might be connected to the plans you have for your future.

REMINDERS

- Stay focused on the same single memory from the last few weeks.

- Reflect as deeply as possible on your thoughts and feelings, how the event has affected your life, and how you hope it will affect your future.

- Take time to feel proud of your openness, strength, and hard work from the beginning.

Writing Session 5 Prompt

From Written Exposure Therapy, by Sloan and Marx, 2019, Washington, DC: APA. Copyright 2019 by the APA.

Today is the last session. I want you to continue to write about your feelings and thoughts related to the traumatic event and how you believe this event has changed your life. Remember that this is the last day of writing, so you might want to try to wrap up your writing. For example, you might write about how the traumatic experience is related to your current life and your future. As with the other writing sessions, it is important for you to delve into your deepest emotions and thoughts throughout the session.

Before you begin writing:

1. Check-In: How distressed are you feeling in this moment before writing? (0 = not at all, 10 = the most I ever felt)

2. Set your 30-minute timer, and when you're ready, begin your timer and begin writing.

If you need more space to write there are a few extra pages at the end. Once time is up, please remember to measure how you feel below.

Post-Writing Check-In: How distressed are you feeling in this moment?
(0 = not at all, 10 = the most I ever felt)

Take a moment to transition your mind from the memory to reflecting on your writing experience. Ten minutes is about the right
amount of time for the next section. If you need to, ground yourself
in the present moment by using each of your five senses to notice
something about the room you are in, or refer to Appendix A for
more techniques.

Wrap-Up and Transition

Writing reflection: How did the writing feel? What was difficult or challenging about it? Did you remember more than you expected? Remember: do not continue writing about the memory; reflect only on the writing process itself.

CONCLUDING NOTE

From Written Exposure Therapy, by Sloan and Marx, 2019, Washington, DC: APA. Copyright 2019 by the APA.

As I've stated previously, you will likely have thoughts, feelings, and visual images concerning the trauma during the course of the upcoming week. It is important that you allow yourself to have these thoughts, images, and feelings, whatever they might be, rather than trying to push them away. Please try to allow yourself to have whatever thoughts, images, and feelings that come up.

Final Note From a Therapist

To engage in this writing for five weeks required great commitment, strength, and resilience. Take a moment to acknowledge this.

Now, we encourage you to take some time to reflect on how things may have changed. Feel free to make any notes on the following two pages or in the back.

- What have you learned about traumatic experiences and its impact on your life?

- What have you learned about yourself?

- Are you engaging in your life—work, personal endeavors, and relationships—differently?

- Do you feel less anxious or agitated?

- Reflect on your Subjective Units of Distress (SUDs) scores over time. What were they in your first and last writing sessions?

WHERE TO GO FROM HERE

We hope this process has helped improve your anxiety and avoidance. We also hope you have learned a new skill and writing practice you can revisit and use whenever you'd like.

If you continue to have difficulty engaging in life or do not see a decrease in your SUDs scores over time, you have options.

You do not have to limit yourself to five sessions. You may continue scheduling weekly sessions for yourself, working with these five journaling questions. If you choose to do this, remember to focus on writing about the moment in time that has most haunted you, being vivid in your description of the event, and digging deep for the thoughts and emotions you had at the time.

If you do not wish to continue writing, want to pursue a different kind of treatment, or are experiencing other symptoms such as depression or substance abuse, consider reaching out to a mental health professional who can provide specialized assessment and personal treatment. We have listed some options for you in Appendix C.

The healing journey is understandably littered with obstacles as we encounter difficult, new truths about ourselves and our world. Regardless of your outcome, we hope you remain encouraged that there are tools out there, and researchers are investigating promising new methods every day. Change is possible, and your continued effort makes it so.

A   Distress Tolerance Techniques

These techniques have been adapted from another highly trusted evidence-based treatment called Dialectical Behavior Therapy, which is helpful for regulating strong emotions. You may consider using these techniques to help ground yourself after your writing sessions or during stressful moments in your life. You can learn more about DBT in Additional Resources.

TECHNIQUE 1: TAKING A MOMENT

In a moment of high distress, we tend to be reactive. We feel compelled to do something—anything—even if we don't know what to do, how to do it, or whether it will be helpful. We rarely take a moment to stop, to breathe, or to think clearly about our next step. If we do, we might find the moment of high distress easier to tolerate.

To Take a Moment

- Take a break from what you are doing. Put the pen down and push the notebook away. Get some mental and physical distance from the thing that is causing such high distress.

- Take a breath. Bring your attention to your breath. Breathe in slowly for 5 counts. Exhale slowly for 5 counts. Repeat for 1 minute.

- Once you feel calmer, think about the most effective next step. Can you return to the task at hand, or do you need to take a longer break and come back later?

TECHNIQUE 2: COOLING DOWN (AND SLOWING DOWN)

Our body temperature tends to run hot when we are in distress. Cooling and slowing down our body can actually bring down the intensity of our emotions.

To Cool Down, Slow Down

- First, splash ice cold water on your face or grab a bag of frozen peas or ice and place it on your face. Do this for about 30 seconds. Notice your body temperature start to cool.

- Next, concentrate on slowing down your breath. Try to intentionally exhale for longer than your inhale. Breathe in for 4 counts, and out for 5. Do this for 1 minute.

TECHNIQUE 3: 5 SENSES

Using our 5 senses to soothe ourselves can help us navigate toward a calmer state. Notice what sensations (sounds, sights, etc.) are making you feel more calm and soothed.

To Soothe with the 5 Senses

- Sight: What can you look at that will help soothe you? Is there, for example, a favorite piece of art, a pet, or a pleasing color or shape you can see?

- Smells: What can you smell that will help soothe you? Is there a lotion, scented candle, essential oil, or familiar scent you enjoy?

- Sounds: What can you listen to that will help soothe you? Do you prefer music that matches your mood, or helps induce a different feeling?

- Taste: What can you taste that will help soothe you? Is there a treat, drink, or snack that you can savor?

- Touch: What can you touch that will help soothe you? Is there something soft, fluffy, and squeezable nearby, or something with lots of textures and ridges you can feel?

B   Frequently Asked Questions

Q: *I've shared this story with therapists, friends, and other people repeatedly, and my symptoms are still here. What's different about this?*

A: When you've told the story previously, it is likely that there has been some kind of avoidance occurring. This might look like giving a cold, factual account of what happened, glossing over your experience in the moment, or describing your feelings, but not experiencing those feelings as you share them. This written format allows you to delve into your experience, feelings, and thoughts in the moment, sharing them honestly and fully with yourself. This allows for the processing and integration of the event and memory.

Q: *How do I pick what to write about?*

A: Start by writing about the memory or event that provokes the greatest distress for you or that you tend to avoid the most. You want to write about a memory that you can recall well, but you don't need to remember it second-by-second. There is also additional guidance in the Preparation section toward the beginning of the book.

Q: *I feel really anxious, nervous, and jittery just thinking about writing, and I haven't even started! What do I do, and what if it gets worse?*

A: This reaction is to be expected and is the result of approaching something you've typically been avoiding. What you are feeling and thinking right now is the fear response being provoked and telling you to go the other way. Take a moment to breathe, calm your system, and recognize that while your body is doing its best to try to protect you, writing about the trauma experience will be beneficial for alleviating these symptoms.

Q: *What if I've experienced multiple traumatic events, or realize there's a different event I want to focus on?*

A: Pick the memory that elicits the greatest sense of distress and avoidance. However, if you have already completed two writing sessions, continue working with the memory with which you began. You have the opportunity to go back through the writing exercises using another memory.

Q: *What if I'd like to stop because it's feeling too difficult or stressful?*

A: To some degree, feeling high levels of distress means the writing is working (even if you start tracking a 9 or 10 out of 10 on your Subjective Units of Distress (SUDs)). Stopping early may reinforce avoidance behavior since it reinforces the pattern of thinking, "I'm not able to experience this distress."

　　　　However, sometimes it may just not be the right time for us to feel this and it's okay if you just don't feel able to continue. If you choose to pause, we encourage you to get back to it as soon as you can and feel ready to.

Q: *What if I'm dissociating?*

A: If you notice that you are feeling disconnected from your body or self, that is
         great awareness. From there, you can practice intentionally reconnecting. Physi-
         cally ground yourself by hanging onto your table, or gripping your chair. Begin
         noticing your present environment—what do you see, smell, hear, taste, touch?

Q: *What if I feel too distressed after writing and feel like I can't cope?*

A: Feeling highly distressed after writing is very natural and is a sign that you were
         engaged deeply in the memory. You may find it helpful to have a transitional
         activity from your writing sessions. This could be a quick walk, having a snack,
         listening to music, etc.
              If you're feeling highly distressed, feel free to practice one of the
         grounding techniques in Appendix A. If you are experiencing suicidal thoughts
         or strong urges to self-harm, please dial 911 or 988.

Q: *What if symptoms start to increase between writing sessions?*

A: It may feel concerning to experience an uptick in symptoms and distress during
         the week, but this is a normal reaction, particularly after the first few writing
         sessions. You are beginning to confront deeply difficult experiences you may
         have been avoiding for a while. See if you can allow these difficult thoughts and
         feelings to surface instead of pushing them away or avoiding them.

Q: *My SUDs rating is low all the time. What does this mean?*

A: Your SUDs rating indicates and tracks how you feel as you practice engaging in
         the trauma memory. Low SUDs (1-3) scores at the beginning of a writing session
         can indicate that this memory is not or is no longer a highly distressing memory
         to recall. If you have low SUDs scores when starting the first or second writing
         sessions, then this memory may not be the one that is fueling your symptoms.
         Try to focus on a particular memory that is more distressing and engage deeply
         with your thoughts and feelings.

Q: *I'm feeling a lot of distress and have a high SUDs score at the start and end of writing.*
        Is this supposed to happen?

A: A high SUDs score is typical in the beginning couple weeks of writing sessions,
        as you are engaging in a distressing memory you've likely been avoiding.
              If you are ending with a high SUDs score (8–10), then this can indicate
        that you have been letting yourself remember and feel the traumatic memory.
        However, if it continues to be rated highly at the end of multiple writing
        sessions, it is possible that you may be overly focused on the moments leading
        up to the traumatic moment, causing your anxiety to increase as you prepare to
        focus on the event. In your next writing session, try writing about your experi-
        ence through the end of that memory.
              SUDs scores tend to decrease over the course of the writing sessions,
        both at the start and end of the writing session itself. If your score hasn't changed
        after several weeks or is increasing over the course of the writing, consider
        options in Appendix C, which may include reaching out to a professional.

C   Additional Resources

FOR PROFESSIONAL ASSISTANCE OR THERAPY:

If you have insurance, try calling or visiting their website to check your coverage. They often provide lists of clinicians covered by your plan.

- PsychologyToday.com is a great search engine where you can find clinicians based on modality, speciality, and what insurance they take.

- OpenPathCollective.org is a non-profit that helps provide affordable therapy for middle- and lower-income individuals and families.

Tip: It may be helpful to call a few different clinicians before choosing.

FOR MORE ON WRITTEN EXPOSURE THERAPY:

- *Written Exposure Therapy for PTSD* is the official treatment manual (we thank the APA for copyright permissions and license).[8]

- "Brief Novel Therapies for PTSD: Written Exposure Therapy" (Thompson-Hollands, Marx, Sloan 2019) provides a great overview.[7]

FOR MORE ON PROLONGED EXPOSURE THERAPY OR
EXPRESSIVE WRITING:

- The American Psychological Association has a great page
  on Prolonged Exposure Therapy that features Dr. Edna
  Foa's work.[15]

- *Opening Up by Writing it Down* (Pennebaker 2016) is a
  thorough and easy-to-read book on expressive writing
  written by the founder.

FOR DIALECTICAL BEHAVIOR THERAPY AND MORE
DISTRESS TOLERANCE TECHNIQUES:

- *The Dialectical Behavior Therapy Skills Workbook* (McKay
  2019) is one of the most well-known and used workbooks
  for DBT.

- LinehanInstitute.org is a non-profit founded by the creator
  of DBT.

References

[1] American Psychiatric Association. (2013). *Diagnostic and statistical manual of mental disorders (5th ed).*

[2] *How to manage trauma.* National Council for Mental Wellbeing. (2022, February 9). Retrieved July 19, 2022, from
▸ *https://www.thenationalcouncil.org/resources/how-to-manage-trauma/*

[3] LeDoux, J. E. (2014). Coming to terms with fear. *Proceedings of the National Academy of Sciences*, 111(8), 2871–2878. ▸ *https://doi.org/10.1073/pnas.1400335111*

[4] Quirk, G. J., Armony, J. L., & LeDoux, J. E. (1997). Fear conditioning enhances different temporal components of tone-evoked spike trains in auditory cortex and lateral amygdala. Neuron, 19(3), 613–624
▸ *https://doi.org/10.1016/s0896-6273(00)80375-x*

[5] Van der Kolk, B. (1998). Trauma and memory. Psychiatry and Clinical Neurosciences, 52(S1). ▸ *https://doi.org/10.1046/j.1440-1819.1998.0520s5s97.x*

[6] Rauch, S. L. (1996). A symptom provocation study of posttraumatic stress disorder using positron emission tomography and script-driven imagery. Archives of General Psychiatry, 53(5), 380.
▸ *https://doi.org/10.1001/archpsyc.1996.01830050014003*

[7] Thompson-Hollands, J., Marx, B. P., & Sloan, D. M. (2019). Brief novel therapies for PTSD: Written exposure therapy. Current Treatment Options in Psychiatry, 6(2), 99–106. ▸ *https://doi.org/10.1007/s40501-019-00168-w*

[8] Sloan, D. M., & Marx, B. P. (2019). *Written Exposure Therapy for PTSD: A brief treatment approach for mental health professionals.* American Psychological Association.

[9] Phelan, H. (2018, October). What's all this about journaling? The New York Times. Retrieved December 1, 2021, from
▸ *https://www.nytimes.com/2018/10/25/style/journaling-benefits.html*

[10] Pennebaker, J. W. (2017). Expressive writing in psychological science. Perspectives on Psychological Science, 13(2), 226–229.
▸ *https://doi.org/10.1177/1745691617707315*

[11] Sayer, N. A., Noorbaloochi, S., Frazier, P. A., Pennebaker, J. W., Orazem, R. J., Schnurr, P. P., Murdoch, M., Carlson, K. F., Gravely, A., & Litz, B. T. (2015). Randomized controlled trial of online expressive writing to address readjustment difficulties among U.S. Afghanistan and Iraq War Veterans. Journal of Traumatic Stress, 28(5), 381–390. ▸ *https://doi.org/10.1002/jts.22047*

[12] Sloan, D. M., Marx, B. P., Lee, D. J., & Resick, P. A. (2018). *A brief exposure-based treatment vs cognitive processing therapy for posttraumatic stress disorder: A randomized noninferiority clinical trial.* JAMA psychiatry. Retrieved July 19, 2022, from ▸ *https://pubmed.ncbi.nlm.nih.gov/29344631/*

[13] Kross, E., & Ayduk, O. (2011). Making meaning out of negative experiences by self-distancing. Current Directions in Psychological Science, 20, 187–191.
▸ *http://dx.doi.org/10.1177/0963721411408883*

[14] Kross, E., & Ayduk, O. (2017). *Self-distancing: Theory, Research and Current Directions*. In J. Olson (Ed.), Advances in experimental social psychology (Vol. 55, pp. 81–136). San Diego, CA: Elsevier Academic Press.

[15] American Psychological Association. (n.d.). *Prolonged exposure (PE)*. American Psychological Association. Retrieved July 19, 2022, from
▸ *https://www.apa.org/ptsd-guideline/treatments/prolonged-exposure*